Transmissions

By Chris Bird

Edited by
Naino Masindet and Tom Mallender

Write-London.com

Write-London is supported using public funding by Arts Council England via Grants for the Arts and the National Lottery.
It is also supported by Creative Future.

1st Edition

Transmissions

Authors Note -

"Most of these poems and stories are related to a time in 2008 when I was homeless in London while dealing with undiagnosed Schizophrenia. During this time, I entered a period of substance abuse. Since my diagnosis I have spent time in crisis houses and hospitals. I attend Art Therapy groups and day centers as often as I can."

Chris Bird – Spring 2023

Editors Notes-

"This project has been a joy to be a part of, and just as much a real eye-opener into the realities of homelessness, addiction and mental health. A massive thanks to my mentor Tom for the opportunity to be part of this project for my editing debut. And thanks to Chris for trusting and allowing us to shape his story."

Naino Masindet – Spring 2023

"I have had the pleasure of knowing and working with both Chris and Naino for a number of years as part of the Write-London collective. Assisting Chris to tell his story, in his words and to bring to life the London he experienced while in the twin grip of undiagnosed schizophrenia and heroin addiction has been one of the most rewarding and artistically interesting which I have been a part of. It has been a true joy working with Naino as my co-editor and sounding board on this project as we interpreted and navigated Chris's unique and personal work.

This book could not have been produced without the two of them."

Tom Mallender - Spring 2023

This book was published with the assistance and support of
Write-London

Contents

Heroin Will Mislead You

Wastage

Blood Moon

Rush

Road to Nowhere

Saints

Devoured

Face to Face

Bloodshot

Enigma

There I Go

Puppet

Snatched

They Came from The Shadows

Crowds

Our Side

Turn to Stone
Therapy

It looms over you like a friendly giant, with devious intent

Smoke

I

I thought about the city skyline.
Tower blocks, spires, skyscrapers and domes
scratched out on the side of a lit cigarette.
Grey shadows became ashes, wide swerving entities
of smoke stretching away like autobahns.
If you watch the embers long enough,
the strength of heroin overwhelms.

II

I pulled out a broken fag from my pocket.
Laid some cardboard on the pavement and sat.
The traffic choked the wide avenue.
Tube stations gorged on commuters.
Junkies filling up with grey smoke.
This was my skyline.

Street Signs

Polluted air billowed around me
as I cut across the road.
Hoardings advertised long-gone movies.
Darth Vader looking out through grime
reminded me of an interstellar Satan.

Beside an open iron gate
bins were over flowing.
Under some crude graffiti,
I noticed a discarded syringe:
a street sign.

I was in the right place.

Jim

My friend Jim radiated criminality.
It was in his gestures.
It was in his movements.
He was the one stopped.
He was the one searched.
He claimed he got police hassle
because
He was Glaswegian.

To me, he seemed heroically resilient.

The Plan Was to Beg

I craved nicotine,
beneath it a growing shadow.
I waited hesitantly beside the kiosk.

From glossy covers,
elegant slim models stared.
Whispers scattered about me,
fragments of conversation.

Anxiety nearly overcame me.
The cravings stirred.
I itched from skinhead to dirty trainers.

I had to sit.

Even in Summer, Pavements Are Always Chill

I sat on a folded piece of cardboard;
this was crucial
sleeping in wet trackies is a nightmare.

The slow pattern of commuters began to increase,
dark faces lit by station lights.

Jim had bullied me into it.
He knew what would be taken.
No fooling him by swiping a few quid.

He advised me that 80% of "scrapnel"
came from commuter women,
Muslims the more generous.

My trainers were grey with dirt, so was the pavement.
Jim always commented,
"London is dirty inside and out, a cruel git."

The Dear Green Place

Jim portrayed Glasgow as a dilapidated paradise.
Where sudden, unpredictable bouts of drunken fury
punctuated the days of rain.
He loved Scotland with a visceral adoration,
Ibrox stadium, his nirvana.

Transmission

Heroin travels easily from stations and ports, it finds its
way into the world with infinite tentacles through flats
onto street corners and estates.

Small time dealers, sometimes heavy users, are the
mechanical element in the conspiracy of distribution.

Gear transcends normal concerns, mortgages, rent, bills.
Trainers, no longer a status symbol.
Heroin casts itself above all such everyday concerns.

Community

Much of the time I felt lonely,
confused and anxious.
I yearned to fit in.

So,
I took the risk of buying smack in Kings Cross
for Jim and Sal.

For a time,
I belonged.

The Walk

Even in summer,
King's Cross looked bleached and grim.
The walk back to Lincoln Inn Fields
was going to be a challenge.
The gear was in my left sock,
it was hard to believe it took a crumpled £50 to get.

I noticed a sticker on a lamppost,
a white 'A' symbol on a black/red background.
Anarchist concepts had always attracted me,
but I had become apathetic in the grips of gear.
My days now defined by the search for smack
or the cash to buy it.

I recognised a girl who haunted King's Cross.
She must have guessed that I was 'holding'.
"A yu gona be a pal?" she hissed.
I hurried past,
lending a thumbs up gesture that fell empty.
I heard her curse me in the distance.

When I reached the park I was pouring with sweat.
My t-shirt stuck to my skin,
I wanted to tear it off.
The park was too busy, every bench full.
I could see my tent in the distance.
I was nearly there.

Our Park

On one side of our park lay a concrete path lined with wooden
benches, the other, high spiked railings. They ironically provided
us with a certain amount of security. There was an old dilapidated
bandstand which attracted alcoholics at night because it was partly
protected from wind and rain. We preferred to stay in ragged tents
in the bushes.

Jim scratched a single word on a nearby bench:
"Saints".

Hush

Outside the park, I walked in a daze.
Unmedicated, hearing murmurs around me.
I made flaying, wheeling strokes
with my arms like a crazed windmill.

A "hush" technique I'd learnt.

The voices abated.
They soon showed up again.
Leaping down from branches,
catching me in their web:

"88 slide."
"Invisible remote control."
"You hate them."
"So far for what?"

Forsaken

I felt flat, abandoned.
Contained in an aching space of silence
as silver heroin ghosts faded.
The ground seemed unsteady under me.

My mouth tasted like machinery.
I sat down on collected cardboard,
in an alley off a side street,
dark and piss stained.

I had to sleep.
Tiredness gnawed at me,
I heard crows call out.
There was rain in the air.

Loose Change

I begged outside the Catholic Church
close to the park where we had our tents.
"Any loose change please" my mantra.

Jim scrawled on a ragged bit of cardboard
with a run out marker,
"Money for Hostel."

The spelling so bad
it might as well have been Martian.
The money was not for a hostel.

Smack shocked my undiagnosed schizophrenia
back into hiding.
Unsettling voices receded.

I still heard old London ghosts
who watched and waited for me to make an error.
I begged to feed my thirst.

Gift

Sally and Jim argued from their tent late into the night.
Their battles were vicious,
extended bouts of cutting verbal abuse.
These rows were sparked by rattling comedowns.
Arguments establish pecking orders.
Jim was simply unbeatable.
On her own Sal couldn't have survived long,
Jim had dragged her into addiction.

Slow Motion

Jim gave me a cigarette.
A sordid blessing from a corrupt priest.
I needed confidence,
it was my turn.

"Go Superdrug, get something pricey,"
he ordered.
I was pants at thieving,
scruffy and self-conscious.

I skirted around the perfume boxes,
bound with grenade-like tags.
In front of me were rows of deodorant.
That wouldn't impress Jim.

The staff were distracted,
the moment would soon pass.
I took a box,
anticipating a blaring alarm.

On my return, I braced myself
to show Jim what I had nicked.

"Toothpaste!" He spluttered derisively,
looking angry then bursting into laughter.
"And it was on special offer, you clown!"
He smiled with ragged teeth.

Secret

As the evening darkened, the proclamations began.
In high rooms above dirty streets, radios spoke
in a series of denials and denunciations.
Unrelenting whispers between bursts of static interference
beamed silver and white into the spaces
between flowers and trees.
Neon patterns dazzled the evening sky.
People scratched their heads perplexed
and gestured to the skyline.

The voices read from gravestones and tabloid headlines.
Anniversaries of wars and triumphs fused with endless lists
of letters and secret codes.
Prayers collided with incantations.

City maps were blurring. The words and whispers defined
an abyss of waiting.

Sanctuary

Heroin looms over an addict
like a psychotically single-minded ghost.
For street users, it distorts reality.

Hurrying gaunt figures with cheap mobiles
hunt their source of utopia.
A sheltered spot from watching eyes,
small quantities traded for crumpled notes.
It's always fleeting.

Eating, keeping clean, even warm,
are far down the list of needs.
It's seedy, yet the hit is ethereal brilliance.

The city
wraps itself
around you
in an
unwelcome

Heroin Will Mislead You

Sometimes
the warm glow of satisfaction
lasts for hours.
Loneliness negated, solved.
Aspirations cooled and reduced
to the miniature concept
of scoring again.
Heroin is a demanding drug.
It's jealous.
Devouring heart and soul,
it is the best and worst.

Wastage

Jim was aghast at the waste
involved when smoking heroin
as opposed to its intravenous use.
Though I usually deferred to him
my phobia of syringes kept me smoking.

Shooting up carries obvious risks.
Veins collapse in arms,
soon the addict shoots into:
legs, hands, groin, toes,
even eyeballs and anywhere.
Blood clots and ulcers plague the sites.

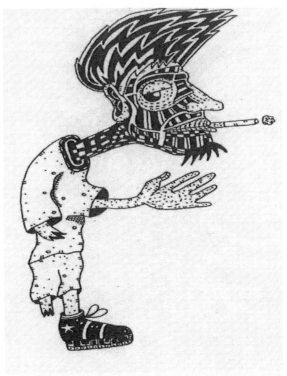

Blood   Moon

On a dirty bench in a city park
I felt beyond fear.
Feelings of inadequacy faded to nothing.
All too soon the sense of elation
descends into sliding discomfort.

The sky darkened.
My skin prickled, itched.
My empty body called for more.

Rush

I lay back on the mattress. A stretch of silver paper caught a strand of sunlight. It was difficult to catch my breath. It was as if a pillow was pressed over my face. I gripped my hand slowly to encourage the surge of ecstasy in my chest. A warm ocean of comfort filled my guts spreading rapidly along my thighs. My muscles relaxed and I could breathe more easily. The tent seemed strangely distant. I felt myself settle into soundless delirium. I smiled. The sensation dulled, slowly dissolving. Nothing left but a chill emptiness. My heart beat with a dreadful weight. My scalp itched; my mouth tasted metallic. In crushing desolation, I was wide awake. The tent looked at me with a squalid reality. I reached into my pocket, pulled out the small bag.

I thought I had more left.

Road to Nowhere

Near the station there was always a collection of junkies and homeless people, more of whom seemed to appear at dusk. As the working day descended into shadow, the Gothic towers only added to the gloom as traffic remained relentless. Neon lights shone in gaudy colour above people waiting, cigarette smoke trailing. I embraced their degeneration and self-loathing.

I never envied the suited and booted, the mortgage dependent, the rent slaves; all constrained and defined by work. Their footsteps hit the grey pavements as they rush from office computers or congested sandwich bars. The sense of exclusion is double edged.

Sitting in an alcove watching the Victorian station could seem the most wonderful experience after using. Traffic noises and passing trickles of chatter provide a fleeting background. People walk by usually discussing TV, food, shopping or sports, sometimes a snatch of politics.

In the distance, a police siren showed London was still alive. The yearning to score was already rising inside me but bearable for now. Tomorrow?

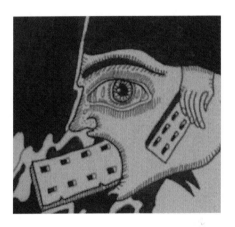

Saints

Jim had a habit,
humming,
"The Saints are Coming", a song by The Skids.

An old punk band from Dunfermline.
He knew every word,
always rasping out the lyrics.

Facing hurdles and disappointments with
recklessness or purpose.

Heroin does that.

Devoured

I stared out waiting for Jim to arrive.
The park was quiet, office workers had headed home.
I sat on the bench while gear soothed every concern,
I let it consume me, and my useless scraggy body.

The comedown appalled my insides.
The urge to vomit and a flu-like feeling now consumed me.
Cigarettes were tasteless, unsatisfactory.
I tried to reassure myself, soon gear would reignite me.

Face to Face

I

All around the darkening street whispers
intermingled with swiftly moving faces,
each spilled expressions.

The glow of shop fronts issued fleeting promises.
Sounds distorted by street lights.
Brakes whined and engines growled threats.

II

I felt weak.
Withdrawal.
A wave of nausea.
My bones ached.
Out of the moving crowd of shadows
I recognised Jim's swagger.
He leant down close to me and winked.

watch with disdain

Bloodshot

As I reached town
a voice spiralled,
stopping me in my tracks.

"Some people hate you," he whispered,
"they can kill you!"

"Cameras… everywhere…" I responded.

Enigma

Cryptic links connect
objectively unrelated words
in an unsettling pattern:

Telephone, Elephant.

These nouns
signifying separate formal meanings
are linked when I see them.

Hospital contains the malign word *pit*.
Medicine encompasses the negative term *sin*.
Holborn responds to the concept *burn*.

Lion. Liar. Zion.
Treat. Trick. Tie.
Con. Crown. Can of Cola.
Tan. Tarantula. Taint.

There I Go

As I held out the packet,
Jim looked with ferocity at my offering
in the gloom of the tent.
He snatched it,
slumping onto the dirty mattress.
"You can fuck right off!" He growled.

He'd sent me,
ordered me really,
up to Kings Cross to buy smack.
On the walk there I lost a tenner,
throwing away our hard-begged money.

As I walked in the park I felt utterly alone.
A street lamp projected a dirty-yellow light.
I wanted to step into that discoloured glow
and disappear.

Puppet

A reluctant vein bulged beneath pale skin
as I pulled the cord on his arm.
In his hand the syringe looked clean, harmless;
a throwaway indiscretion.

"Ok," said Jim.
For a moment everything froze.
He backed into the mattress and closed his eyes.
A trace of blood along his pale arm.

I sat back and lit a fag, looking at Jim.
A skinny mannequin doll,
laying in an odd, ungainly position.
His legs kicked out involuntarily.

He started mumbling, struggling to get up.
I offered him my cigarette.
I could taste nicotine on my lips as I whispered,
"Now me."

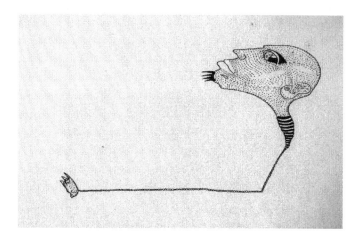

A future

without

light

Snatched

Clambering out of my sleeping bag,
I craved a cigarette.
I knew I had none.

The flap to Jim's tent was open.
I looked at his pale hands as he slept.
In his right, he held a small packet.

I snatched it in a second.

I found a vein behind my left knee.
My arms were useless.
I shot it all.

Delirium.
The city responded with radio babble.
Colours streamed from flying crows.

Jim still slept.

They Came from The Shadows

Like a chav light brigade, they charged.
Cursing booze-muddled words.
In that moment the evening shattered.

The attackers as young as joyriders,
vindictive as Nazis.
Brave with cheap lager and speed.

I caught a glimpse of white trainers
kicking at the flimsy tents.
The tents gave up easily.

In a whirl of bitter giggles and drunken bravado,
The attackers were gone.
Silence.

Crowds

One after another, they came out of the mist.
Face after face moved with pale regularity.
In the background neon lights glowed.
Shadows moved between the faces.
The streets sighed.
The city was troubled.
The procession never ended.

Words jumped like tiny white flames
amongst the faces.
TV aerials caught discarded sayings,
spoken in strange mazes.
"Here we fall, here we fade".
Still the crowds came,
crowds and shadows together.

Our Side

Fluorescent orange waistcoats loaded the lorry.
They cleared the tents without looking at us,
muttering to one another.

Jim and I stood on the path, a pathetic air about us.
Jim, Sal and I'd been staying in the park for months.
We'd been given the tents by a Hindu charity.

The park warden watched like a cut-price lieutenant
overseeing the eviction. A distracted police officer
stood beside him, they both exuded disinterest.

"Crunch" went the tents as they folded in on themselves.
Our camp disposed of as if litter.
A murder of crows screeched, disturbed by the upheaval.

So much time to overcome

when

you have nowhere to go

Turn to Stone

The first revulsion is the smell.
Incarcerated men fart, spit, shit,
piss, cough and throw up.
The days fade one after another
without a glance at the horizon.
The muffled cries of the young
catch your attention at first.
Men with little or nothing to lose
are at once both pathetic and menacing.
Demons line the wing walkways.
Forlorn monsters with colds and coughs
brought on by withdrawals are a sad sight.

A special cell is set aside for the first taste
of imprisonment.
When the metallic cell door closed
I listened to my own heartbeat.
I stared at my palms.
They were pale and damp.
I heard a whisper.
A spiral sequence of voices advised me
that the Jewish elders had murdered Christ.
In the distance, heavy doors slammed shut.

I fear the night
The seven times Christ spoke on The Cross
The remote stars reveal the city's bleak heart

Therapy

Harriet spoke to us like a primary school teacher approaching recalcitrant kids. She was the new art therapist on the ward. Nurses had been encouraging patients to attend all morning. Our primary focus was lunch but 5 or 6 of us had joined the group in the day room.
She exuded liberal kindness.
Nathan beside me at the table stank of piss. An all-pervading pungent aroma. I couldn't move seat. The plastic chairs, like the tables, bolted to the floor. The narrow ward windows were also secured.
Had a fight once develop over the merits of watercolour compositions.

Paul looked uneasy, fidgeting in his chair, glancing at me. He had a ruthless streak when provoked.
Mohammad sat opposite. He was a timid, emaciated character who could not stand up for himself in an empty room. He was being bullied on the ward.

"Can we have music, Miss?" Paul rumbled in a deep voice.

"No fucking way!" snapped Andrew.
Andrew claimed to be a gangster, a dealer.
Insisted we refer to him as 'Cobra'. The natural rival to Paul.
Harriet smiled to encourage peaceful co-existence. Looking at her, I genuinely hoped no one kicked off.
I tried to smile back in a gesture of muted reassurance.

Paul shuffled, assessing the degree of threat from Cobra.
Once satisfied, hurled a plastic jug of water.
It sailed across the table, missing him but drenching Harriet.

On The Ward

Spring was detained beyond the dull glass.
I spent most of my days in my room on a thick immovable
mattress.

The new patient, Dominic, stood in the TV room. A suede jacket
decorated with a peace badge, with his floppy fringe, his expensive
watch, his very poshness had annoyed every soul on the ward. It
was rumoured he was stealing but I doubt he needed to. He had
entered another patient's room.

Paul loomed over everyone dressed in a grey blanket. When
annoyed, he banged the desk at the nurse's station. He reminded me
of a giant, scary child. He spoke with a crazed smile.
"You wanna git a big, long rest in ta garden," he repeatedly told me
like a psychotic doctor from a nightmare.

"Ok," I replied, noticing one of his wrists bandaged.

Paul refused to eat the "muck" served in the ward kitchen. He left
dragging his grimy blanket on the polished floor.

Mohammad, it seemed, was grateful for every morsel. He ate as if
every meal was his last.

Outside I could see birds fluttering around a pond in the garden. I
always counted them.

Paul was an eagle, wild but wounded. Mohammad, an owl, subtle
and cautious. And I, a caged robin lost. Wrong season, wrong
time, a bird who has forgotten how to sing.

Soon we were all complicit in a murder plot.

Tom stood in the doorway to my room, needing cigarette papers. His pasty white face gaunt and menacing, in a pathetic junkie way. I regarded Tom as a potential threat. He had done a lot of bird up in Pentonville.

"Only nicked for gear," he had explained.

I tossed him a half a packet of Rizlas. He left without a word.

All was quiet until a large group of orderlies appeared near the nurse's station. It was very sudden. They reminded me of undertakers or security at a club.
The mass surged towards Paul's door. He opened it slowly, as if he knew. His eyes had lost their potency. Framed by the door of his room he looked captive, "escorted" to a more secure ward.

Thus ended the murder plot, the authorities having gotten wind of Paul's plan to neck Dominic.
I never saw either of them again.

I was soon alone in my cell-like room. Around my wrist a plastic band with my name and NHS number.

Slowly each day, the feathers came emerging from the skin of my hands and shoulders. I kept this discovery hidden knowing it was the key to my escape

Dimming

I was nothing special
trapped in between city pavements and parks
sedated by antipsychotic medication.

Graffiti on street corners and tube trains
spoke in tongues to me
beneath the frenetic skyline.

I conveyed invisible invitations to the twilight
while I faded
in my own unique descent.

Unrelenting Hunger

Antipsychotic medication
bloats the human shape
in a distinct and irreversible manner.
Plump faces and swollen bellies
commonplace in wards and day centres,
-zapine's leading to overeating.

Rainy Day

Grey skies loomed above London.

The crawling traffic showed my bus's arrival was a distant hope. A bit of clumsy graffiti caught my attention: "Stranger Danger." The phrase seemed very deliberate to me. Could it be an accident?

From the window of a passing van, a song came to me sang by David Byrne of Talking Heads.

My thoughts reflected on the graffiti and the lyrics, loosely linking the two. "Road to nowhere stranger, Danger!" Associations jumped to mind implying violence, futility and my place in the street.

I heard a voice from behind me:
"Stranger in Bethlehem manger. Stranger dead!"

I remembered the psychiatrist had suggested that when I felt unwell to find a peaceful spot away from people. Easier said than done.

"Bus stop strangler."
"Damn good morning."
"Crap take!"

I knew this voice. Just as a crow's screech scares away other birds, it dominated other voices.

There was now an elderly man in a raincoat at the bus stop. He looked smart, despite holding an empty carrier bag.
He stared at me.
Why doesn't he look away? I thought.

He stared while the voices swirled around me. He stared and stared, stepping toward the busy road just as my bus arrived.

TV

Channels started relaying information, especially to me, in a variety of devious ways. A character in *Doctor Who* whispered to me: "You are 77."

"77" could signify that I should have died in 1977 and thus did not deserve benefits.

A newsreader sighed, warning me:
"Capricorn no Pepsi."
I deduced as a Capricorn, Pepsi was particularly bad for me. I always loved it but attempted to give it up.

Robin Hood was a show I watched regularly, was unsettled to discover that the hero hated me specifically.
"Cesspit", the name he gave me.
Batman said nothing.

Watching *On the Buses,* a detached piece of dialogue spelled out:
"You didn't give your Mum enough food. You ate it all yourself!"

It made me ruminate about my deceased Mum. I rationalised, "She was very thin. Had I forgotten to give her food? Aren't elderly people generally thin?"

In the background the TV staggered on with underhand pronouncements.

The grim shadows casting spells and trouble slowly filled each day. I stayed indoors 24/7.

A washing machine advert whispered I should give up food and drink.

I entered a slow dive world of damage and despair. I couldn't block the words.

I talked about these experiences with Doctor Medley, a compassionate doctor. Auditory hallucinations, caused by the symptoms of schizophrenia, this explanation helped.

I listened to Bowie loudly on earphones. I was advised this would help from someone on the ward.

"Jean Jeanie" rattled into my head.

Persistence

The bus rattled and shook as it approached Camden Town. Some bright spark had outlined the letters 'WHUFC' in the grime on the window. I imagined the dirt on their finger after tracing this celebration of West Ham United Football Club, my dad's team. It's my team.

I began to mull this over.

Why had I sat beside this particular window on this particular bus? Had someone anticipated my presence? Publicised my allegiance? Was it possible local newspapers or radio stations were involved or was there perhaps a wider conspiracy?

As I thought of radio stations, a significant association suggested tube stations.

Camden contained the hidden word "m*ad*". Den means "*from*" in Turkish, my second language. "*From mad*" sounded like "*fromage*" which means "*cheese*" in French. Although these mental links and associations were slight and subtle, they reverberated from a web of entangled thoughts.

I looked at my trembling palm, its network of wrinkles mirroring my fragmented thoughts.

The sluggish progress of the bus emphasised my own snail-like movement through each day.

Welcome

A week-old newspaper lay on the table in the dingy day room. I reached for it and settled into the least busy corner browsing now old Parliamentary scandals.

Opposite me, the kettle wheezed its way to boiling like an old car revving up. A service user rang the buzzer from the outside gate waiting to be let in by a volunteer.

The psychology students who made up the pool of volunteers on the main had a kind and yet lost quality.
They floated around greeting people with affected warmth.

"Cup of tea or coffee?" They asked as more people appeared heading towards the boiling kettle.

The far corner was Joe's corner. He fancied himself a boxer, swivelling and air punching quick jabs with little hisses of effort. Some days he stripped off his t-shirt, today fully clothed. Weaving from side to side he threw a big right hook. Another knockout victory.

In the corner by the window, it was kicking off. A dispute about someone sleeping on the sofa.

"Do one you idiot!" The formerly sleeping woman shouted.
"Have a cuppa and shut your trap," someone suggested.
"Keep ya nose out!" Came a barked reply.

An argument was boiling. I turned the page.

Structure
Tea and coffee are a light bulb
to the moths of mental illness.

Tea bags and tablespoons of instant coffee
pinned the empty hours to the structure of the day.

Moths to a Flame

The day center opened at 11, meaning service users hung around waiting in nearby cafes or the church yard. The intercom never worked and probably suffering from its own mental instability. The heavy entrance gate near immovable. Volunteers would press enter and lights went out in the office.

Inside, if you ever got there, was a drab and dejected social area decorated with photocopied notices for The Walking Group to Kings X or a Hearing Voices Workshop. A blackboard beside the door listed daily activities. Partly out of frustration and boredom, I added events to the blackboard: Group Excursion to Beachy Head, the Pensioner Wrestling Focus Group, How To Sign on in 42 Different Places (including Cardiff) Workshop, and a group simply titled "Hitler Studies", for which there was a genuine enquiry about.

Service users on worn-out sofas examined newspapers with glazed expressions. They'd shuffle toward the small garden to smoke roll ups. Everyone chain-smoked, a probable consequence of zapine dependency.

I left after lunch, there was always a gloomy lull then.

The iron gate seemed reluctant to let me out. Muscle-bound weightlifters would have struggled with it, let alone us unfit service users. Perhaps this indicated we had no easy access to the real world.

Printed in Great Britain
by Amazon

34425113R00044